# Earth, Sun and Moon

## Contents



## About this unit

In this unit children are introduced to the facts that the Earth, Sun and Moon are spherical, that they differ in size and are a great distance apart. They learn that although the Sun appears to move across the sky during the day, it is, in fact, the Earth that moves and spins, and that we experience day and night as a consequence. Sunrise and sunset are discussed along with the variation in length of day. Children learn that the Earth takes a year to orbit the Sun and that the Moon orbits the Earth over 28 days during which it appears to change in shape.

**Scientific enquiry** is planned into the unit and focuses on:

- obtaining and interpreting evidence using tables and graphs.
- drawing conclusions; comparing and explaining conclusions.
- recognising that evidence cannot always be directly obtained and that the work of others needs to be considered and assessed.

# Background Scientific Information

For many reasons, teaching about the Earth in space is not easy. Children come to school with their own ideas about space; and some of those ideas are very difficult to dislodge. They may believe, for example, that the Sun moves and the Earth stands still and, given that the Sun appears to move across the sky, this is understandable. Although this idea was questioned by Copernicus and later disproved by Galileo, the movement of the Sun rather than the Earth was accepted science until the fifteenth century. Other commonly-held misconceptions include: the theory that the Moon covers the Sun at night; that the shadow of the Earth is what causes the apparent change in shape of the Moon; and that the Earth is further away from the Sun in the winter (when, in fact, the opposite is true for the UK).

The National Curriculum restricts teaching about astronomy at Key Stage 2 to the Earth, Sun and Moon (although few schools can resist the temptation to teach about the other planets, too). There are three important concepts to tackle:

### Firstly, their difference in size.

The Earth, Sun and Moon are all spherical, which is a function of the force of gravity which pulls all matter towards the centre of an object. Because books usually need to fit all three into a small picture, we have little idea of their relative sizes. A million Earths could fit into the Sun, and the Moon is only one-sixth the size of Earth. The differences in size are, literally, astronomical.

### Secondly, the distances.

If you model the Sun with a beach ball, the Earth is about the size of a pea and the Moon the size of a peppercorn. At these sizes the Earth and Sun are 40 metres apart. The Sun is our nearest star. The next star, on this scale, is 4000 kilometres away – on the east coast of Canada.

### Thirdly, the relative movements.

The Sun is actually moving and spinning, together with the whole solar system and the galaxy. But for the sake of simplicity, let us imagine it is still. The Earth orbits it – the great Copernican discovery – and, as it orbits, the Earth is spinning. Both orbit and spin are anticlockwise; the orbit gives us our year and the spin gives us day and night.

As the Earth orbits the Sun, the Moon orbits the Earth. Since the Moon always has its face turned towards us, the back of the Moon (often incorrectly called the 'dark' side) is constantly away from us. For this to happen, the Moon has to spin as well as orbit, and its rotation and orbit are synchronised. The Moon's orbit is not in the plane of the planets and, since it bobs up and down, it can appear in different places in the sky at different times (and during both day and night, though it is usually blotted out by the Sun's brightness).

The Moon is not a light source. Instead, it reflects the Sun's light and it is this, together with its orbit, that makes it appear sometimes as a full Moon and sometimes as a new Moon (plus all the phases in between).

With these three concepts understood, the relation of Earth, Sun and Moon should become clear.

# Information and Communication Technology

Where appropriate, ideas for ICT opportunities are included throughout the Teacher's Notes. The table below indicates where ICT skills could be developed in this unit.

| Task | ICT Opportunity |
|---|---|
| **4** The sunniest room | *Use a temperature sensor and graphing software. Research using CD-ROMs and the Internet.* |
| **10** Changing daylight hours | *Research using CD-ROMs and the Internet.* |
| **11** Modelling the Earth's orbit | *Research using the Internet.* |
| **12** Facing the Earth | *Use DTP to draw a diagram.* |
| **Checkpoint 2** | *Design a web site.* |

# Scheme of Work:

| Learning objective: Knowledge and understanding | Task | Learning objective: Skills | Literacy and numeracy links | Resources and safety | Evidence of learning Children: |
|---|---|---|---|---|---|
| | **1 What do you know about the Earth, Sun and Moon?** Children revisit things that they that they know or believe to be true about the Earth, Sun and Moon. | Understand that not all evidence can be collected first-hand. | Reading with understanding. | **Safety!** Remind the children of the danger of looking directly at the Sun throughout all this work, whatever the time of day. | Can understand that the Sun is a star and that it gives us heat and light; that the Earth is a planet and that it is made of rock, air and water; and that the Moon is made of rock and that nothing lives on the Moon. |
| The Earth, Sun and Moon are spheres. You cannot test things directly, but you can learn from what others found out. | **2 It's a round world.** Children draw and write their ideas for how they would prove the Earth was round and not flat. | Realise that sometimes you can't test things directly, but that you can learn from what others have found out. | Reading non-fiction. | **Task sheet 1.** | Can recognise that the Earth, Sun and Moon are spheres.<br>Can understand the importance of evidence. |
| The Earth, Sun and Moon are very different in size. | **3 Just how much bigger?** Children experiment with spheres to appreciate the different sizes of the Earth, Sun and Moon. | | Writing, justifying. | Spheres of different sizes (beach ball, football, watermelon, tennis ball, table-tennis ball, orange, marble, peas, round bread, seeds peppercorns). | Realise that the Earth, Sun and Moon are very different in size. |
| The Sun appears to move across the sky through the day. Different things can be discovered from the same evidence. | **4 The sunniest room.** Children record how sunny a room is at different times and on different days. **5 Hazel on the train.** Children use pencils to simulate visually the movement of the Earth and Sun, and how this affects our perception of which is moving. | | Handling data. | Thermometer, temperature or light sensor (optional). **Task Sheet 2.** Graphing software. CD-ROMs and Internet access. Three pencils. **Safety!** Warn the children against looking at the Sun as permanent damage can be caused, in rare cases, without any initial pain. | |
| The Earth spins on its axis every 24 hours. | **6 Street scene.** Children compare two pictures, one night-time and one daytime. **7 Spinning Earth.** Children use a torch and sphere to simulate how the Sun shines on the Earth. | | Reading comprehension. | Bright torch, globe or a large ball, tiny piece of Blu-tack. **Task Sheet 3.** | Can understand that the Earth spins on its axis every 24 hours, and that this rotation gives us day and night.<br>Can recognise that the part of the Earth facing the Sun is in daylight; it is night in the part facing away from the Sun. |
| | **Checkpoint 1.** Children give reasons to explain some common misconceptions about the Earth, Sun and Moon. | | | | |
| | | | | | |

| Learning objective: Knowledge and understanding | Task | Learning objective: Skills | Literacy and numeracy links | Resources and safety | Evidence of learning Children: |
|---|---|---|---|---|---|
| The Sun rises in the east and sets in the west.<br>Observe the pattern in the Sun rising and setting. | **8 Turning Earth. 9 Back-to-back spin.** Children work in groups or pairs to 'act' out the Sun and Earth and their rotations. Using a torch, they then work out what happens during the day and at night. | Observe the pattern in the Sun rising and setting. Represent observations as a graph. | | Space to carry out these activities safely, bright light. Safety pins or sticky tape, card. | Can observe and model that the Sun rises in the east and sets in the west.<br>Can graph their observations or secondary data as a graph. |
| | **10 Changing daylight hours.** Children draw graphs of sunrise and sunset times for certain days in June. | Data handling. | Numeracy, data handling. | **Task Sheets 4,5,6.** Graph paper (optional), calculator (optional). Internet access. | |
| The Earth takes a year to orbit the Sun. | **11 Modelling the Earth's orbit.** Children work with a partner to model the orbit of the Earth around the Sun. | | | Space to carry out this activity safely. Internet access and CD-ROMs. | |
| The Moon takes about 28 days to orbit the Earth.<br>The Moon looks different during the course of a month because of its orbit. | **12 Facing the Earth.** Children enact the roles of the Earth and the Moon and their respective orbits. | | | DTP software. Shoe box, black paint and brush, scissors or hole punch, polystyrene ball or table tennis ball, wire, torch. | Can explain why the Moon appears to change shape. |
| | **Checkpoint 2.** Children investigate misconceptions about the Moon. Children design a postcard or web site showing the most interesting facts they have learned about the Earth, Sun and Moon. | | Literacy, select and evaluate information. | Web page maker. | |
| | **Summary.** Children read through the statements and complete the **Science Log.** | | | **Science Log.** | |
| | **Assessment Tasks.** Children do structured tests to assess their knowledge, skills and understanding of the Earth, Sun and Moon. | | | **Assessment Task Sheets A and B.** | |

# What do you know about the Earth, Sun and Moon?

TASK 1

## Purpose

This Task revises what children should already know about space and provides an insight into their ideas. They should be clear that:

- The Sun is a star. It gives us heat and light. It is not made of rock.
- The Earth is a planet. It is made of rock, air and water.
- The Moon is made of rock. Nothing lives on the Moon.

These concepts were covered by the original Star Science Infant resources; and they are common to children's 'space' understanding.

Questions are suggested below to establish the children's understanding of these ideas. If you find that their grasp of the concepts is weak, then you will need to reinforce this learning as these concepts underpin everything they will learn in this book. Another important point to establish is the importance of secondary data since it is not possible to investigate space at first hand. Children must learn instead to research and to evaluate evidence collected by others.

## What to do

Ask the children what they know about the Earth, Sun and Moon and be prepared for some pretty staggering – and sometimes inaccurate – answers. A good way of structuring this kind of question is to use a concept map. Children write the words 'Earth', 'Sun' and 'Moon' on a large sheet of paper with lots of space between. They then join the words with linking lines and statements. For example, a line from Earth to the Sun could have the words 'goes round' along it.

One refinement of the technique is to use more than one colour for the lines. You might use one colour for known facts and one for 'thought' ideas, such as 'I think there is no water on the Moon'.

Discuss the finished maps. You or the children might like to keep them until this unit is complete. You can then look back and see what has changed and what the children have learned. As a class, you might like to finish the unit by correcting the information on the old map or by drawing a new and accurate one.

| QUESTIONS | *Possible answers* |
| --- | --- |
| ◦ What do you know about the Earth, Sun and Moon? | |
| ◦ What shape are they? | *Balls or spheres.* |
| ◦ What are they made of? | *The Earth and the Moon are made of rocks. But the Sun is made of hot gases.* |
| ◦ Do they move in space? In what sort of path? | *The Earth and Moon move both in orbit and by spinning.* |
| ◦ What happens to the Sun during the day? | *It appears to move across the sky.* |
| ◦ How does the Moon change during a month? | *It appears to get smaller then larger again.* |

## Watch out for!

There are many misconceptions to look out for as you proceed through the unit. (The commonest ones are listed under each activity.) Remind the children of the relation of the four cardinal compass directions and encourage them to learn them off by heart.
**Safety!** Remind the children of the danger of looking directly at the Sun throughout this work, whatever the time of day.

TASK 2

# It's a round world

### Purpose

For children to understand that the Earth, Sun and Moon are all spheres and to learn that it is not always possible to test things directly but that you can learn from the discoveries of others.

### What to do

Eratosthenes, a Greek poet and scientist, is credited with first concluding that the world is a sphere. His calculations of the size of the Earth were remarkably accurate.

Ask the children to read the story of Eratosthenes and to suggest ways (which are given in the **Fact File**) of persuading others that the Earth is a sphere. They should use **Task Sheet 1** and the principal arguments should include:

- You can travel round the world.
- When ships appear over the horizon, they come over a curve. You first see their masts, then their funnels, and lastly the hull.
- When there is an eclipse of the Moon, the curved shadow of the Earth is cast on the Moon's face.
- The Earth is a planet. We can see that other planets in space are not flat.
- Pictures from artificial satellites show that the Earth is a sphere – it is the shape of a ball.
- We can also see that the Moon is a sphere from satellite images.
- Scientists can prove using theories and measurements that the Sun is a sphere.

### QUESTIONS

- What shape is the Earth?
- How do you know?
- What evidence is there for its shape?
- Do you think this is good evidence? Why?
- Why did people might think the world was flat?
- How would you persuade them otherwise?

### Watch out for!

The Earth isn't, in fact, a perfect sphere. It is flattened very slightly at the poles.

TASK 3

# Just how much bigger?

### Purpose

For children to recognise that the Earth, Sun and Moon are very different in size.

### What to do

Ask the children to choose different sized spheres, from a range you provide, to show the relative sizes of the Earth, Sun and Moon. Your collection of spheres will depend on what is available, but try to find a wide range from a beach ball or watermelon to a small bead, round seed or similar.

The enormous difference in size between the Earth, Sun and Moon should be emphasised. If the Sun is a beach ball, the Earth is a pea and the Moon is a peppercorn. The question of why the Sun and Moon look alike in size may be raised and you may want to discuss relative distances. The relative sizes of the Sun and Moon, and their relative distances from us, are related mathematically. This is why they appear to be the same size.

Many children will remember the total solar eclipse of summer 1999, when the Moon covered the Sun completely, and this is a good discussion point to draw the children's attention to the relative sizes of objects when viewed from different distances.

### QUESTIONS

- Choose something to represent the Earth, Sun and Moon. Think about their sizes. Why did you make that choice?
- Why do the Sun and Moon look the same size from Earth?
- What else is large but looks small at a distance?

### Watch out for!

One common misconception is that the Earth, Sun and Moon are very similar in size and research has shown that children will draw all three about the same size. This misunderstanding is not helped by books that necessarily place all three on the same page, not to scale, or by some models which are used for teaching.

# The sunniest room
# Hazel on the train

TASK 4-5

## Purpose

For children to learn that the Sun appears to move across the sky through the day and to appreciate that it is possible to discover different things from the same evidence.

## What to do

The **Fact File** on page 8 presents the work of Copernicus and Galileo and draws the children's attention to how scientific evidence can change people's ideas.

Tasks 4 and 5 are related to the issue of the relative movement of the Earth and Sun. The evidence of our eyes – the apparent movement of the Sun and the changing length and direction of shadows – supports the idea that the Earth is motionless and that the Sun orbits it. Task 4 focuses on how the Sun appears to move, while Task 5 introduces a simple model for the children to try to demonstrate why it appears that the Sun orbits the Earth rather than vice versa. Children could record their results from Task 4 on **Task Sheet 2** or use ICT. They may need to use a new sheet for each room.

The Extra Challenge gives the children the opportunity to discover more about Copernicus and Galileo. The **Fact File** and diagram on page 10 explain that the Earth also spins. This is addressed in Tasks 6 and 7.

| **QUESTIONS** | ***Possible answers*** |
|---|---|
| • Which is the warmest room in the school? | |
| • Which is the warmest place to sit in our classroom? | |
| • Is that true for both the morning and the afternoon? | |
| • Why is it warmer at one part of the day than at another? | |
| • Which way does the Sun appear to move? | |
| • What compass directions are those? | *From east to west.* |
| • Which is moving – the Earth or the Sun? | *The Earth.* |
| • How can we see the Sun appear to move when we know that the Earth is moving and the Sun is standing still? | |

## Watch out for!

The most obvious misconception is that the Earth is standing still and that the Sun is moving, and the evidence of our eyes confirms this to us. It is not unreasonable to expect children to take some time to grasp the scientifically accepted truth – after all, it has only been confirmed a few centuries ago! Millions of people lived and died under a 'moving Sun'.

Another confusion that can arise results from any shadow stick activity. The shadow moves in the opposite direction to the Sun, from west to east. **Safety!** Warn the children against looking at the Sun as permanent damage can be caused, in rare cases, without any initial pain.

## ICT OPPORTUNITY

Children could use temperature sensors and graphing software to record their data.

# Street scene
# Spinning Earth

TASK 6-7

### Purpose

For children to learn that the Earth spins on its axis every 24 hours and that this rotation gives us day and night. They then go on to appreciate that the part of the Earth facing the Sun is in daylight; the part facing away from the Sun is in darkness – night-time.

### What to do

Begin Task 6 by discussing the changes of day and night. Emphasise that this is a cycle – that it repeats and will go on repeating. Let them look at the differences we can see between day and night. In Task 7 the children see that the Earth is spinning in front of a powerful light source and facing that light source will bring us into daylight, and turning away from it will bring us into night. Ask two children to come to the front and stand back to back or if you have the space, the whole class in pairs. Both children represent the Earth – one of them is in the UK, the other in Australia. Shine a light towards them (a table lamp, a strong torch or even the window light). Tell the class that one of them faces the light – they are in the day – and the other faces away – for them it is night. Ask them to move round on the spot, staying back to back. For accuracy, they should turn anticlockwise.

The model of Earth with its bit of Blu-tack, confirms that the night to day transition is caused by the spin of the Earth. Remind the children as they carry out this activity to turn the Earth anti-clockwise. The **Fact File** contains additional information on the Sun and how we are able to see the Moon, this information can be difficult to grasp and may need additional explanation. It is supported in Task 12.

### QUESTIONS

| QUESTIONS | *Possible answers* |
|---|---|
| How are night and day different? What differences can you list? | |
| What do you know about the movement of the Earth? | *It spins anti-clockwise.* |
| The Earth is turning in front of a light source (the Sun). What will that do to the shadows on the turning Earth? | *They will change size and direction.* |
| What do we call the shadowed and lit parts of the Earth? | *Night and day.* |
| How are day and night connected to the turning Earth? Tell me how this appears to you. | |

### Watch out for!

Children may assume a self-centered purpose for the night, such as 'It is night because we need to sleep', or they may confuse cause and effect, for example 'It is night when it gets dark/when the street lights come on/when I go to bed'.

Other issues may arise from children who have travelled long distances by aeroplane. If they have travelled from east to west, to the USA, for example, they will have travelled with the Sun, and the day will have stretched on interminably. Tackle this in the next teaching section, after Checkpoint 1, when they look at the direction of the Sun's apparent movement.

## CHECKPOINT 1 Seeing the light

Ask the children to answer all the questions in the activity using the concepts they have learned so far. You are looking for answers along these lines:

**Question 1:**

Some reasons that prove the Earth is not flat are:

- *When ships appear over the horizon, they come over a curve. You see their masts first, then their funnels, and finally the hull.*
- *When there is an eclipse of the Moon, the curved shadow of the Earth is cast on the Moon's face.*
- *The Earth is a planet. We can see that other planets in space are not flat.*
- *Pictures from artificial satellites show that the Earth is a sphere – the shape of a ball.*
- *Eratosthenes showed that the Sun's light did not shine down all the Earth's wells simultaneously, which it would do if the Earth were flat.*

There are other pieces of circumstantial evidence to do with travelling and circumnavigation.

**Question 2:**

*You might tell the children that their results certainly suggest that the Sun is moving and the Earth is still, but you could point out that they would get the same effect if the Earth were moving and the Sun standing still. The trouble is that they are making their observations from a moving planet. They must use evidence gained by scientists such as Copernicus and Galileo to support their answers.*

**Question 3:**

*A person on Earth can see the Moon because it reflects the light of the Sun. They see it because for them it is night-time, and the Moon is clearer in the night sky than during the day.*

Children draw their ideas on **Task Sheet 3**. They may need help in deciding where the arrows depicting light from the Sun will go and perhaps in deciding where the Sun is in the picture.

**Watch out for!**

Remind the children that the Moon is not a light source. Some may think that the Moon will always be in the Earth's shadow as it is in an eclipse of the Moon. The picture hugely collapses the distances between the Earth, Sun and Moon. Children should be clear that in reality, the distances are so great that the shadow of the Earth rarely coincides with the Moon. Remember to tell children to depict light as a straight line.

# Turning Earth
# Back to back spin
# Changing daylight hours

TASK 8-10

### Purpose

For children to learn that the Sun rises in the east and sets in the west, and to know how to observe the pattern in the Sun rising and setting. They then learn how to graph the changes in daylight times by using 'day length'.

### What to do

You will need a large, shaded open space for the Tasks 8 and 9, the 'circle' activities. Both provide an excellent practical experience that leads to greater understanding, and it is worth making the effort to do them. If you provide one-sided light by opening a blind or curtain, so much the better. Another alternative is to use a table lamp or strong torch as your light source. When doing these Tasks, ensure that the children move anticlockwise (as seen from above). If they do not do this, they will find it difficult to understand the apparent east to west movement of the Sun.

The table given in Task 10 and on **Task Sheet 4** shows the changes in sunrise and sunset times through June 2000. Similar tables can be found for any month of the current year on meteological and weather web sites. If they are listed in GMT an extra hour should be added for BST. Children may not have been introduced to these differences at this stage and this may require additional explanation.

For simplicity, the table below lists one date in each week of June, 2000. From these, the hours of daylight (BST) can be calculated:

| Date | Sunrise | Sunset | Hours of daylight |
|---|---|---|---|
| 1st | 04:49 | 21:08 | 16 hrs 19 min |
| 8th | 04:45 | 21:14 | 16 hrs 29 min |
| 15th | 04:43 | 21:19 | 16 hrs 36 min |
| 22nd | 04:43 | 21:21 | 16 hrs 38 min |
| 29th | 04:46 | 21:20 | 16 hrs 34 min |

The longest day is 22 June – the summer solstice. Daylight hours increase ('days lengthen') up to this date, and reduce ('days shorten') after it. Using the Internet, children can explore the whole year pattern. They will see how daylight hours change, and may come up with the winter solstice, the 'shortest day of the year'.

**Task Sheet 5** has a blank graph format for recording the data but more able children could draw their own graph using squared paper or ICT.

Using **Task Sheet 6**, the Extra Challenge enables them to broaden their research by focussing on different cities in the UK.

**QUESTIONS**

- How do the daylight hours change?
- Which day has the most daylight hours?
- What happens to daylight hours before/after that day?

**Watch out for!**

One way to understand the complex issues involved here is to consider the all-day breakfast. Suppose the children wanted to go on eating breakfast all day. How could they do it? They would have to be in each country of the world at breakfast-time – and that would be possible if they followed the Sun around the Earth, arriving in each country in the early morning. If they have travelled west by air, they will have experienced this. If they have travelled east, the day will have been collapsed, and the evening meal comes up too fast!

Try not to talk about changing 'day length', day length itself does not change – it always stays at 24 hours. The hours of daylight, however, do change, and children are aware of the ways in which these changes affect their lives.

TASK 11

# Modelling the Earth's orbit

### Purpose

For children to learn that the Earth takes a year to orbit the Sun and understand that it may not be possible to measure the length of a year directly.

### What to do

The **Fact File** discusses how difficult it is to measure a year. In today's world, there are plenty of annual events, but for the ancient Egyptians, an accurate measure of the year was impossible. Their year was marked by two events coinciding: Sirius, the Dog Star, rising in line with the Sun and the annual flood of the River Nile. This is a case where it is necessary to accept secondary evidence. But children should learn not to accept this evidence without question. They might like to research some of the ways we have of measuring year length. The **Fact File** on page 20 discusses the occurrence of leap years.

The Extra Challenge gives children the opportunity to use the Internet and CD-ROMs to carry out research into how other planets move and their relative positions.

| QUESTIONS | *Possible answers* |
|---|---|
| • What are the seasons of the year? | *Winter, spring, summer, autumn.* |
| • Can you name some annual events? | |
| • Which events go in which season? | |
| • How many days are there between one annual event and another? | *365. (Leap years may arise – see below).* |
| • What is that period (a year) measuring? | *This is how long it takes Earth to orbit the Sun.* |
| • What is the shape of the path the Earth takes? | *An ellipse – virtually a circle, but with the slightest flattening.* |
| • So where is the Earth every year on a particular day (a birthday, for example)? | *The same place, relative to the Sun as last year.* |
| • So what is a year? | *A year is our measure of the time it takes the Earth to orbit the Sun once.* |

### Watch out for!

The elliptical shape of the Earth's orbit can lead some children to think that the Earth is further from the Sun in the winter, and that's why it's colder. In fact, the opposite is true – the Earth is nearer to the Sun in the UK winter. If the seasons were caused by how close we were to the Sun, it would be the same season all over the Earth at the same time – and not winter in Australia when it's summer in the UK. Seasons are caused by the fact that the Earth's axis is tilted as it orbits the Sun. Countries titled towards the Sun experience its direct heat and experience their summer. Countries tilted away from the Sun are heated obliquely and experience their winter.

The issue of leap years may also arise. The Earth takes close to 365 and a quarter days to circle the Sun. This means that after four years it is not in the same position for the date as it was last time – it is one day out. If this creep were allowed to continue, we would eventually end up with the events and seasons of the year moving their way to the wrong weather! So every fourth year we add one day (29 February).

The issue of astrology may arise. There is no scientific basis for belief in astrology, but you may have your own views on whether it is actually harmful. You might also note that some cultures do not celebrate birthdays.

TASK 12

# Facing the Earth

**Purpose**

To learn that the Moon takes about 28 days to orbit the Earth and that this is the reason it looks different throughout a month.

**What to do**

There are many common misconceptions about why the Moon looks different at different times. Some of these are:

- The Earth casts its shadow on the Moon, so it looks a different shape.
- Clouds are covering part of the Moon.
- The shadow of the Sun falls on the Moon.
- Planets cast their shadow on the Moon.

By modelling the movement of the Moon around the Earth, children will learn that this movement, by changing the shape of the shadow on the Moon as viewed from Earth, changes the apparent shape of the Moon itself. They will also learn that the Moon rotates as it orbits. The Moon's rotation is synchronised with its orbit, and this explains why the same side of the Moon faces us all the time.

The Extra Challenge activity is a useful exercise to reinforce this point, but you must make it clear to the children that it is not a perfect model of the phases of the Moon. In the activity, you have to move your head to see the different phases modelled – it is as if the Earth was moving. In reality, the Moon is moving, causing the phases.

You might like to teach children the names of the different phases: New and Full Moon, waxing and waning.

| **QUESTIONS** | ***Possible answers*** |
| --- | --- |
| ∘ What is the Moon made of? | *Rock.* |
| ∘ Is it bigger or smaller than the Earth? | *Smaller.* |
| ∘ Does it orbit? | *Yes.* |
| ∘ Does it rotate? | *Yes.* |
| ∘ How do we know that it rotates? | *Because we only see one side of it.* |
| ∘ Is the Moon a light source? | *No.* |
| ∘ How can we see the Moon? What light is it reflecting? | *It reflects the Sun's light.* |
| ∘ How long does the Moon take to orbit the Earth? | *Approximately 28 days.* |
| ∘ Why does the shape of the Moon appear to change? | *Because we see different amounts of the part that is illuminated by the Sun as the Moon orbits Earth.* |

### Watch out for!

The phrase 'the dark side of the Moon' is confusing. The side of the Moon that faces away from the Earth is not in constant darkness, as will be seen when you do the activities. The 'dark side' is a poetic term – not an astronomical one. The side that faces away from the Earth and is not seen from Earth is known to astronomers as the far side.

The Moon is often visible in the day. On occasions it may be in the sky during the day but it is not visible because of the bright light of the Sun, which blots out the reflected light from the Moon.

The Moon's orbit is not in the same plane as that of the planets. Most of the planets orbit in the same plane – as if they were moving around on a tabletop. But the Moon ducks and climbs through its plane as it orbits. This explains why it appears to be in different parts of the sky each day and night, rather than following the same apparent path as does the Sun.

The Moon has its own gravity which is weaker than the Earth's gravity because the Moon is smaller. This gravitational pull along with that of the Sun is responsible for the tides.

### ICT OPPORTUNITY

Children could use DTP to construct a diagram showing how the Moon orbits the Earth.

CHECKPOINT 2

## Space explorers

Ask the children to investigate the questions. Answers should be along these lines:
"The Moon is flat, Captain. We shall bounce off!"
*The Moon is a sphere, like the Sun and Earth.*

"The Moon is made of cheese, Captain. And what if the little green men get us?"
*The Moon is a rocky ball. It is unlikely that any creatures can live there.*

"We can't fly to the Moon tonight, Captain. Half of it is missing!"
*The Moon appears to change shape through the month – the Moon's phases. But it's all there, all the time! The dark part is in shadow. Sometimes its edge can still be seen, confirming that it is a sphere.*

"We shall miss the Moon for sure. Look at it, Captain. It's tiny!"
*The Moon is smaller than the Earth, with a diameter (and circumference) about a quarter the size. But its apparent small size is due to its distance from us.*

"It will be just as close to fly to the Sun as the Moon. They're both the same size!"
*Both appear the same size in the sky. Although the Sun is hugely bigger than the Moon, it is considerably further away – and so they appear to be identical. The Sun would be far too hot to approach.*

**ICT OPPORTUNITY**

Children could create a web site advertising holidays in space and explaining what attractions could be seen.

S

## Summary

An opportunity for the children to assess their own progress using the **Science Log**. Tell the children to circle the face that best reflects how confident they are with each statement.

## A Assessment Tasks

An assessment of children's learning. Give the children **Assessment Task Sheets A** and **B**. The questions are below, with selected answers in *italics*.

### ANSWERS

1 Imagine you met someone who thought the Earth was flat. "What!" they say. "Your world is a sphere? Prove it!"

Go on. Prove it. Show why we think the Earth is a sphere.

- *When ships appear over the horizon, they come over a curve. You see their masts first, then their funnels, and finally the hull.*
- *When there is an eclipse of the Moon, the curved shadow of the Earth is cast on the Moon's face.*
- *The Earth is a planet. We can see that other planets in space are not flat.*
- *Pictures from artificial satellites show that the Earth is a sphere – the shape of a ball.*
- *Eratosthenes showed that the Sun's light did not shine down all the Earth's wells simultaneously – which it would do if the Earth were flat.*

2 In 1609 Galileo Galilei found evidence to support the ideas of Copernicus. Write what you know about what Galileo proved.

*Galileo proved that the Earth was not the centre of the Universe or, indeed, of the solar system – but that the Earth orbited the Sun. Galileo provided the evidence that confirmed the earlier theories of Copernicus.*

3 The Sun shines on Duncan's computer screen in the morning. But it doesn't shine on it in the afternoon. Tell him why the Sun appears to move across his screen.

*The Earth turns so that the Sun appears to move across the sky, making different rooms sunny in the morning and in the afternoon.*

B

## Assessment Tasks

**1** Louise's phone rang in the middle of the night. "Hello!" said a voice. "It's me, your Aunt Rose, phoning from Australia!" "But Auntie," said Louise. "It's the middle of the night here!" "Nonsense," said Aunt Rose. "It can't be. The Sun is shining."
Explain why Aunt Rose made her mistake.
*It was the middle of the day for Aunt Rose because she was in Australia. Her side of the Earth was facing the Sun, she was in daylight. But Louise was in the UK, on the opposite side of the Earth, and facing away from the Sun. For Louise it was the middle of the night.*

**2** "Why is there usually only one full Moon a month?" asked Kate's little sister. Tell her why the Moon appears to change over 28 days.
*The Moon is orbiting the Earth once every 28 days. As it circles us, we see different views of the lit part of the Moon. These different views make the Moon appear to change shape. The Moon is lit by the Sun, this is why we can see it.*

**3** Nasreem's little brother did not want to go to bed. "It's too early," he said. "The Sun is still shining." "That's because it's June," said Nasreem. "What's that got to do with it?" he asked. Tell him why daylight hours are longer in the summer.
*The Earth is tilted as it orbits the Sun. So the path the Sun appears to take across the sky varies through the year.*
*In the summer, the Sun appears in the sky for longer, and climbs higher. In the winter, the Sun appears in the sky for a shorter time, and does not climb so high. When the Sun takes the higher, longer, summer path, we have more hours of daylight.*

# Task Sheet 1

*Name* ..............................  *Date* ..............................

These children all believe that the Earth is flat.
Think of three pieces of evidence that prove that the Earth is a sphere.
Write and draw to explain your evidence to the children.

# Task Sheet 2

*Name* ..............................................................................................................  *Date* ..................................................

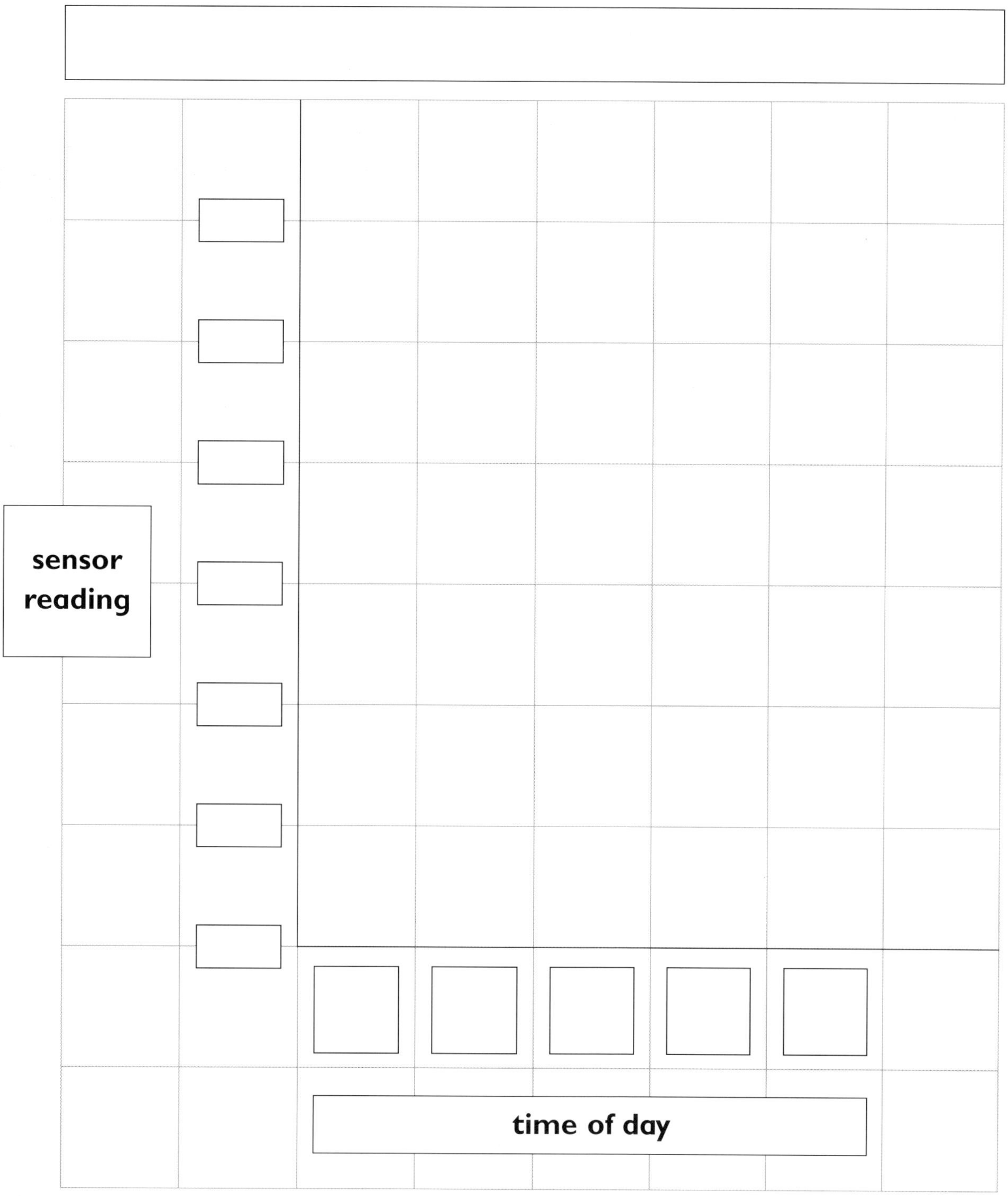

# Task Sheet 3

*Name* ..................................................... *Date* ..............................

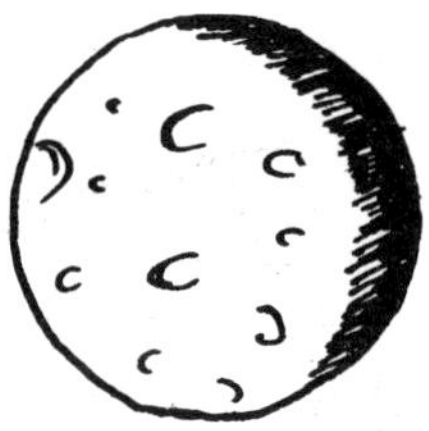

**Moon**

**Earth**

# Task Sheet 4

Name ............................................................ Date ..............................

**1** Draw a graph of sunrise and sunset times for June. Here is a table showing the sunrise and sunset times on one day in each week.

| Date | Sunrise | Sunset |
|---|---|---|
| 1st | 04:49 | 21:08 |
| 8th | 04:45 | 21:14 |
| 15th | 04:43 | 21:19 |
| 22nd | 04:43 | 21:21 |
| 29th | 04:46 | 21:20 |

- You could draw a separate graph for sunrise, and another for sunset. Or you might be able to put both on one graph – perhaps using different colours.
- Put the dates along the x-axis, and the times up the y-axis. You might label the y-axis with minutes only.

**2** From your graph, you will see that the length of daylight time is changing.

Which of the days you have graphed is the longest?

______________________________________________

What happens to the length of daylight time before and after this date?

______________________________________________

# Task Sheet 5

*Name* ........................................ *Date* ....................

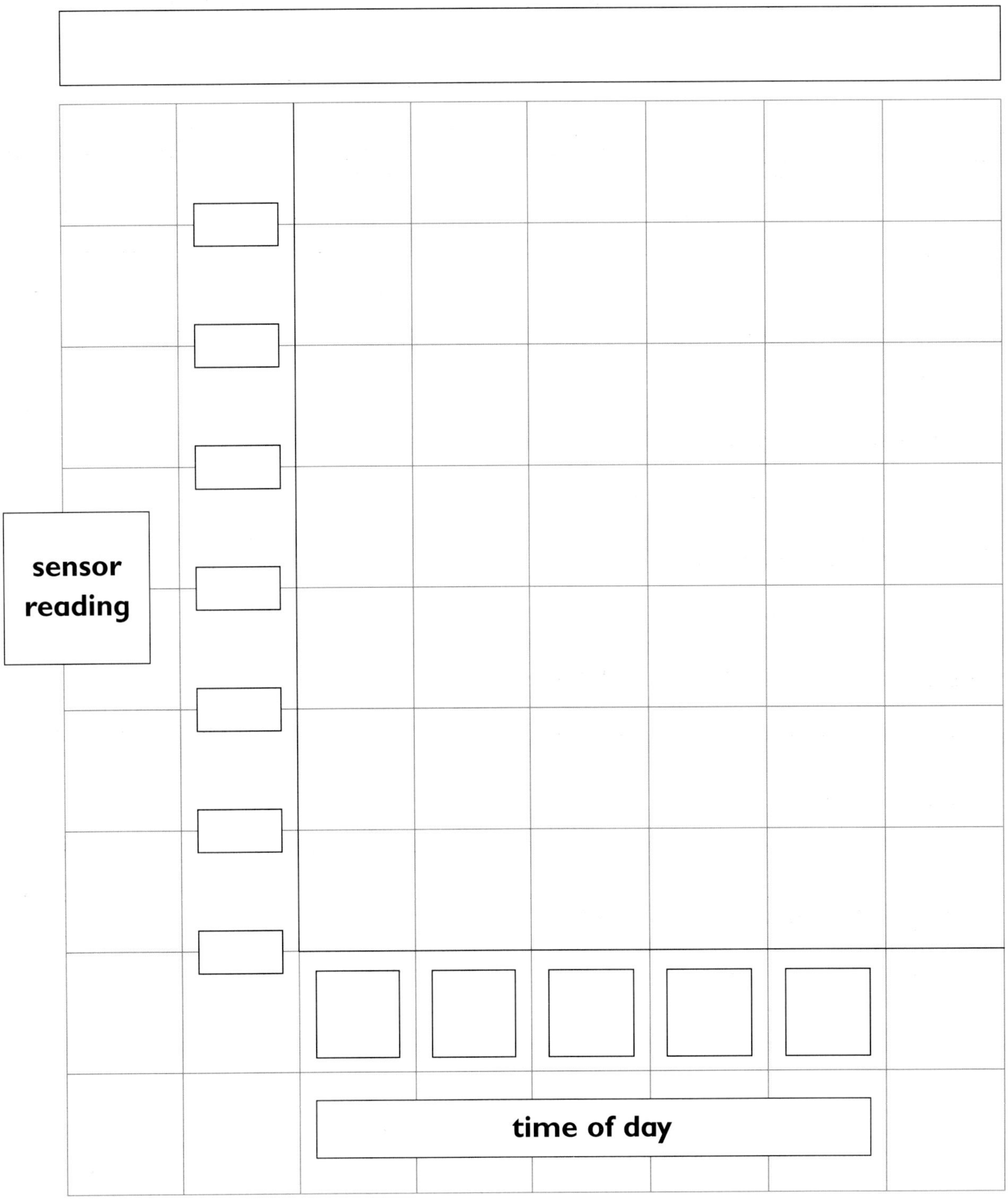

# Task Sheet 6

*Name* ..................................................  *Date* ..............................

**1** Use the Internet to look up the sunrise and sunset times on the birthdays of your friends.

**2** Record their birthdays on this table – or on a computer spreadsheet:

| Name | Birthday | Sunrise | Sunset | Daylight time |
|---|---|---|---|---|
| | | | | |
| | | | | |
| | | | | |
| | | | | |
| | | | | |

**3** Who has a winter birthday?

______________________________

**4** Who has a summer birthday?

______________________________

**5** Who has the most daylight on their birthday?

______________________________

**6** Who has the least?

______________________________

**7** What pattern can you see in the data?

______________________________

# Science Log

*Name* ..................................................... *Date* ..............................

- I know that you can learn from what others have found out when you can not test something directly.

- I know that the Earth, Sun and Moon are spheres that are very different in size.

- I know that the Sun appears to move across the sky through the day.

- I know that you can sometimes discover different things from the same evidence.

- I know that the Earth spins 360° on its axis every 24 hours.

- I know that the Sun rises in the east and sets in the west.

- I know that the Earth takes a year to orbit the Sun.

- I know that the Moon takes about 28 days to orbit the Earth.

- I know that the Moon looks different during the course of a month because of its orbit.

- I can represent my observations on a graph.

# Assessment Task Sheet A

*Name* ..........................................................................................

*Date* ..........................................

**1** Imagine you met someone who thought the Earth was flat! "What!" they say. "Your world is a sphere? Prove it!"
Go on. Prove it. Show why we think the Earth is a sphere.

______________________________________________

______________________________________________

______________________________________________

______________________________________________

______________________________________________

______________________________________________

**2** In 1609 Galileo found evidence to support the ideas of Copernicus. Write what you know about what Galileo proved.

______________________________________________

______________________________________________

______________________________________________

______________________________________________

______________________________________________

**3** The Sun shines on Duncan's computer screen in the morning. But it doesn't shine on it in the afternoon. Tell him why the Sun appears to move across his screen.

______________________________________________

______________________________________________

______________________________________________

______________________________________________

______________________________________________

______________________________________________

# Assessment Task Sheet B

*Name* ..............................................................  *Date* ..............................

1 Louise's phone rang in the middle of the night. " Hello!' said a voice. " It's me, your Aunt Rose, phoning from Australia!" " But Auntie," said Louise. " It's the middle of the night here!" " Nonsense," said Aunt Rose. " It can't be. The Sun is shining."
Explain why Aunt Rose made her mistake.

2 "Why is there usually only one full Moon a month?" asked Kate's little sister.
Tell her why the Moon appears to change shape over 28 days.

3 Nasreem's little brother did not want to go to bed. "It's too early," he said. "The Sun is still shining." "That's because it's June," said Nasreem. "What's that got to do with it?" he asked. Tell him why daylight hours are longer in the summer.

# Curriculum Links

## England National Curriculum

Sc1 Scientific enquiry – *all*

Sc2 Physical processes:

*The Earth and beyond – 4a, 4b, 4c, 4d*

## Northern Ireland Curriculum

Key Stage 2

Investigating and Making in Science and Technology – *all levels*

## Environmental Studies 5-14 in Scottish schools

Earth and Space:

*Earth in Space – levels A, B, C, E*

Energy and Forces:

*Properties and Uses of Energy – levels B, C*

Skills in Science: Investigating – *all*

## Wales National Curriculum

Key Stage 2

Scientific Enquiry – *all*

Physical Processes:

*The Earth and Beyond – all*

# NEW STAR SCIENCE SKILLS LADDER

| | Planning | | | | | Obtaining and presenting evidence | | | Considering evidence and evaluating | | | |
|---|---|---|---|---|---|---|---|---|---|---|---|---|
| | **Asking questions and having ideas** | **Deciding an appropriate approach** | **Planning the detail of what to do** | **Predicting what might happen** | **Choosing what equipment to use** | **Using equipment and carrying out practical work safely** | **Making observations and taking measurements** | **Presenting evidence** | **Drawing conclusions and describing patterns and trends** | **Comparing results to predictions and making further predictions** | **Explaining evidence** | **Evaluating** |
| **Year 4** | Asks questions and offers own ideas for scientific enquiry. | With support knows when to answer a question by using a fair test and when evidence should be collected in other ways. | In a fair test, identifies what to keep the same and with support what to change and what to measure/observe. Plans main steps in other enquiries. Recognises hazards and, with support, plans how to control risks. | Predicts outcomes and sometimes suggests reasons for their prediction. | Selects appropriate equipment and with support, considers the scale and the degree of accuracy required on some measuring equipment. | Uses basic equipment correctly and safely. Begins to deal with equipment failures. | Makes a series of observations. Uses standard measuring equipment for measuring most quantities. | Creates own tables and bar charts. Uses a line chart with support. | Makes a general statement about simple patterns in results. | Makes further predictions from results in simple contexts. | Provides explanations for simple patterns in results. | Suggests how the enquiry might be improved. With support, recognises some of the limitations of their evidence. |
| **Year 5** | Asks questions and offers own ideas for scientific enquiry and, with support, improves question to clarify scientific purpose. | Knows when to answer a question by using a fair test and when evidence should be collected in other ways, including using secondary sources. | Sets up a fair test knowing what to change, what to measure/observe and what to keep the same. With support, considers whether to take repeat readings. With support, plans the detail in other types of enquiry. Assesses hazards and plans how to control risks. | Predicts outcomes and, where appropriate, suggests reasons for their predictions. | Selects equipment from a wider range, including digital scales, forcemeters and computer sensors. With support, considers the scale and the degree of accuracy required on measuring equipment. | Uses a wide range of equipment correctly and safely. Deals with most equipment failures independently. | Makes a series of relevant observations. With support, takes accurate readings on measuring equipment, repeating them where necessary. | Begins to select appropriate way to present evidence. Creates own bar charts and tables, including those for repeat readings Creates a line graph with support. | With support, describes relationships identified, linking both factors and describing whole relationship in comparative terms. | With support, makes further predictions from results and uses these to test out the suggested pattern in the relationship studied. | Sometimes relates patterns in results to scientific knowledge where appropriate. | Identifies how much to trust results. Suggests reasons why similar enquiries yield different results. With support, considers the spread of repeated measurements. With support, recognises some of the limitations of their evidence. |
| **Year 6** | Asks questions and offers own ideas for scientific enquiry which have a clear scientific purpose. | Identifies appropriate approach to answer a scientific question. | Sets up a fair test. Plans the detail in other types of enquiry. Decides whether to take repeat readings. With support, considers whether plans will yield enough evidence for the task. Assesses hazards and plans | Predicts outcomes and, where appropriate, sketches a graph to show the expected pattern in results. Justifies their predictions using scientific knowledge when possible. | Selects suitable equipment for a range of tasks. Takes into account the scale and the degree of accuracy required on measuring equipment. | Uses a wide range of equipment correctly and safely. Deals with equipment failures independently. | Makes a series of relevant observations. Takes accurate readings on measuring equipment, repeating them where necessary. | Selects suitable way to present evidence. Where appropriate, draws up line graph independently, except where scales involve very large or very small numbers. | Describes relationships identified, linking both factors and describing whole relationship in comparative terms. | Makes further predictions from results and uses these to test out the suggested pattern in the relationship studied. | Relates patterns in results to scientific knowledge where appropriate. | Identifies how much to trust results and justifies decision. Suggests reasons why similar enquiries yield different results. Considers the spread of repeated measurements. Recognises some of the limitations |